Vivian & Matt

I know you may never make it to Kar
this is still a nice little bit of what I do. I
work at Nattie's (dlee (#36). It also tells you
a lot about the kind of town this is.
We wish you all the best in your marriage,
and wonderful things to come

♡ Amber & Nathan

The Best Little Coffee Shops In Kansas City

By Sandra Martin

Photography By Isaac Alongi

Published by:

Isaac Alongi, Inc.

Fairway, KS

iastudios.com

ISBN 0-9773849-0-X

The Best Little Coffee Shops in Kansas City

by Sandra Martin

Photography and Design by Isaac Alongi

Printed in the United States of America

Acknowledgments

When I started this project I had no idea what fun it would be. In addition to tasting some of the best coffee in the area, I have had the privilege of meeting some wonderful people. The coffee shop owners were more than helpful and met me with great enthusiasm. Thank you for your help, and best wishes for your continued successes.

A special thank you to my family—to my children, who never cease to challenge me, and my husband, who is a great life partner.

Introduction

This book is for the discriminating coffee drinker. We're not talking about just grabbing something hot with caffeine. You know this book is for you if, when you go to bed at night, you look forward to getting up so you can have your morning coffee.

When you walk into a corporate establishment, you know what you're getting. It's always the same. Although there's something to be said for consistency, those of us who choose a more adventuresome lifestyle and relish the unique find ourselves drawn to the local flavor and friendly atmosphere that comes with a locally owned, beloved coffee shop.

This book is certainly not meant to be an exhaustive guide to all the great coffee houses in Kansas City, but only a few my husband Isaac and I are especially fond of.

HEATHER ELS

If you're looking for a coffee shop where everybody knows your name, this may be the place. Heather, the owner, calls it Cheers without the beers. Even if you're a newcomer, you'll soon feel right at home at this small coffee shop decorated with a South African flair, influenced by Heather's husband's South African roots.

A group of coffee regulars come each morning as much for the company of friends as for the coffee. They even bring their dogs on days when they sit outside and enjoy the fresh morning air.

HEATHER ELS

Heather makes you feel like you're one of the family; if you forgot your money, just sign an I owe you and put it on the wall. This is refreshing, when you find distrust in many places today. Heather says she's only had one person not come back to pay, and she hasn't given up on them yet.

Looking up, you'll see a unique filing system for your coffee club card. For those of us that aren't tall enough to reach the ceiling tiles, there's a little wooden fish on the counter for a more conventional means of filing. There is a friendship garden along the back, where some of the regulars bring plants or flowers from home and transplant them to share with others. But, Heather warns, "We only accept deposits, no withdrawals."

On Saturdays, you can come and make your own waffles. In October, they held their first annual chili cook-off.

When Heather is busy, the regulars just walk around the counter, get what they need, pay, and make their own change. And if you simply can't have your morning coffee unless you have your special mug, just bring it. You can leave it there as long as you wash it, dry it, and put it back where it belongs. Everybody seems to enjoy the casual arrangement; it feels like home.

CHRIS & ELLEN TODD

By the Book offers two of my favorite things: coffee and books. Whether you come for a book or a good cup of coffee, you are in luck. This is a full-blown bookstore and coffee shop located on the historic Liberty Square. They even offer several breakfast selections each morning, like breakfast casseroles, and their yummy baked goods are made in their own kitchen. Bring the kids, there's a whole room full of books just for them, the Children's Nook.

A stairway leads to an upstairs loft with more books. The only problem with this place is that I don't know when to leave.

BOOKS & COFFEE

children's nook

Sara Honan & Jon Cates

Sara opened the Broadway Cafe in 1992. After working in coffee houses during her college years in Chicago, she thought Westport was a great area and chose the Broadway location because of the steady traffic. Jon worked as manager of the shop for a year, before becoming a partner in 1998. Early on, Sara and Jon decided to roast their own beans so they could control the quality of their product. They have since added a second location, just around the corner on Westport Road. You can find them roasting coffee beans there daily. You will also find a full-service espresso bar for carry-out. So if the lines are a little long at the cafe, try their roastery at 301 Westport Road.

When asked about the secret to their successful business, Sara and Jon both agree, they focus on the coffee. For that reason they have very loyal customers.

Parkville is such a fun place to spend an afternoon walking around and browsing interesting little boutique shops. While you're there, visit Parkville Coffee and Fudge, home of the famous Missouri River Bottom Fudge. Get a piece of fudge and a cup of coffee, a wonderful combination.

The coffee shop has been here for over a decade in a great old building, which used to be a market. When I walked in, I got the feeling of walking into an old-fashioned general store. To keep the old feeling of the building Sherry insisted on keeping the old-style espresso machines, even though the guys who keep them working aren't thrilled. In addition to coffee and fudge, you can find all kinds of goodies and local gourmet items. They are great for gifts or just treating yourself.

Americans drink more than 400 million cups of coffee a day.

TOM & DEBBIE ASHBY

f the coffee at Mildred's isn't stimulating enough for you, just take a look around
the fun and interesting décor. Looking up, you will notice painted ceiling tiles created by
ustomers. Some are from a contest, and the others from customers who wanted to leave
heir mark at their favorite coffee shop. You will also see small picture frames all around
lled with photos. I assumed they were of family members. Wrong. According to Debbie,
They're our extended family; they're our regular customers." Debbie gives local
lent an opportunity to display their work by highlighting a new artist each
onth, adding to the eclectic décor.

TOM & DEBBIE ASHBY

Debbie started in the food industry at Gilbert Robinson right out of college, and attributes her attention to customer service and her always striving to do things better to her background in the restaurant business. For example, she makes her own baked goods because bringing them in wasn't good enough.

Over 10 years ago, Debbie decided she was ready to go out on her own and open her own place. She didn't stay on her own for long, since now her husband and three sons all work in the business. Her sons comment that they run the stores knowing it's their family's business and their inheritance—you just can't hire help like that. Mildred's is now in three locations: downtown Overland Park, downtown Kansas City, and the newest shop in the Crossroads District.

22 City Market Coffee Company

Courtney Bates

As a little girl, Courtney came to the city market every Saturday morning with her father. Nine years ago, when her father decided to open the coffee house in the city market, Courtney had reservations about the location, worrying that it would be a weekend-only crowd.

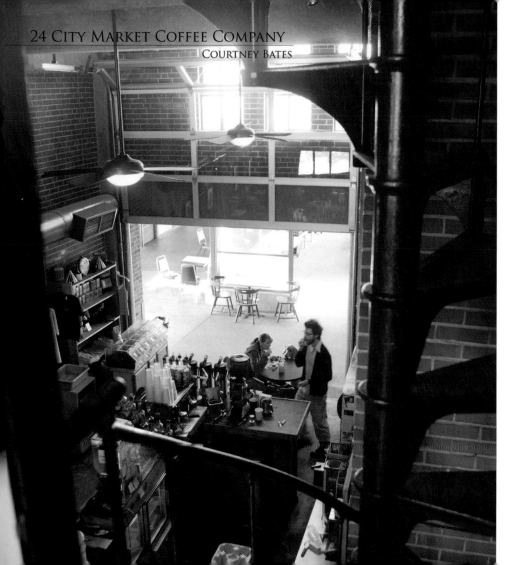

24 City Market Coffee Company
Courtney Bates

During the first years of business things were slow during the weeks and in the winter, when the market wasn't open. But they made it work and felt grateful each spring when they were still there and business would pick up again.

Courtney bought the business from her dad about four years ago and she has been going strong ever since. Soon thereafter, Courtney bought a roaster, and started roasting her own beans. She won the Golden Bean Award in 2001, 2002, and 2003. Today, the environment has changed around the city market with the addition of lofts, apartments and new business developments. So now the regulars live or work close by—it's not just about the weekenders.

Courtney says that from the beginning, they stuck to the belief that it's all about the customer. She also tries to give back to the community whenever possible because she feels the community has supported her business.

Courtney found her future husband at the City Market, so her Dad truly knew what he was doing when he picked that location. As you listen to Courtney talk about her business, you can tell she honestly loves what she does.

At one time in Turkey, during their wedding, men were required to promise to always provide their wives with coffee. If they failed to do so, it was grounds for divorce.

Wine and lemonade merchants in Italy in the 1600s called coffee "Satan's drink" due to its threat to their markets. They asked the Pope to issue an edict condemning coffee. However, their plan backfired when Pope Clement VII tasted coffee, liked it, and baptized it to make it a Christian drink.

English coffeehouses of the 1600s were often a home-away-from-home for many men, who provided the address of their favorite coffeehouse as their own.

At one point during the 1700s, coffeehouses served as barber shops and gambling houses as well as places to socialize.

In the United States, coffee breaks began in industry during World War II as employers learned that coffee increased the productivity of their workers.

T JENSEN

Hi Hat is an example of what can happen when a guy decides to do something he loves. T confesses he comes from a family of coffee snobs. Over the years, as he would romance a cup of coffee, he dreamed of owning his own coffee shop. After learning the coffee industry inside and out by working at the wholesale level, T was anxious to put into action what he had been teaching others to do. He wanted to be on the other side of the business, with the people.

T has five passions in life: his family, faith, sports, art, and coffee. Owning a business centered around one of his loves isn't the only perk; it allows him flexibility. He has two very noble goals, to be a great Dad and to be a complement to his wife. T has had a career in sports broadcasting as well, so it looks like he's been working down the list of things he'd like to do.

In 1999 T found a very unique building for his new venture. Originally a gas station in the 1930s, its most recent tenant had been a hair salon. It took a great amount of vision and creativity to bring the little gas station to what we know it as today. T received an award for the preservation of the building. Many Kansas City coffee drinkers would agree that T has found the best way to use this cozy space, as they make Hi Hat their morning ritual. The change of seasons won't stop them from coming together to chat with friends over coffee. Rain or shine, snow or sleet, they can be seen drinking their coffee on the patio in the morning.

Hi Hat can boast it has some of the friendliest baristas in town. They make a great cup of coffee and make you feel right at home while they're doing it.

T wanted this to be a place where everyone was greeted with, "Hi," no matter who you were or what hat you wore.

DEBRA DETAL

When you walk in the door you may be a little surprised by the decor. It is not your normal run-of-the-mill coffee shop. Lace and all, you're in for a treat. The people are very friendly, which is always important in a place where you might potentially go before you've had your first cup of morning coffee.

It's hard to believe, but I've been told there are some people who like coffee shops, but aren't coffee drinkers. The Coffee House doesn't leave these folks out; they even make drinking tea look fun, like having a tea party when you were little. In fact, there's a separate little section of the shop called the La Te-Da Tea Room—it's just as frilly as it sounds, very Victorian looking.

On one of my visits, a group of four women were playing cards at one of the tables. They get together about twice a month here to play, have lunch, and drink coffee. If you don't have a time set aside with your friends to get together, you can pick up an invitation for just such an occasion, and the invitations are complimentary.
There are plenty of goodies for snacks and for lunch. I was taken with the bubble tea; that was new to me. It's a flavored latte with tapioca balls in it. You drink it and chew it through a fat straw. It was good, but I'm sticking to coffee.

Coffee is the second most valuable traded commodity,
second only to oil.

ROASTING The cooking process that develops the flavors locked in the green beans. Hot air runs through a machine with a spinning drum that tosses the beans.

When roasted, a coffee bean doubles in size, and the caramelization of the sugar turns its color from green to brown.

The longer a coffee is roasted, the more caffeine burns off during the process, therefore dark roasted coffees actually have less caffeine than medium roasts.

When the previous owner of Hattie's, Natalie's mother-in-law Karen Dummermuth, decided that she wanted more free time to travel, Natalie jumped at the chance to take over the business. She was eager to learn everything there is to know about coffee. One of the first things she has been learning, with the help of an experienced roaster, is to roast coffee beans. "Roasting coffee beans is a science and an art," she says. "It's about the way they look, feel, and smell. It's a lot to learn, but when you roast your own beans, you have more control over the quality of the beans. Which, of course, leads to better coffee."

In addition to serving gourmet coffee drinks, Hattie's offers a variety of baked goods made fresh in the store daily. They showcase local artists, and it's a great place to just hang out and read a book or to do a little work on your laptop, but as Natalie says, "the customers keep coming back because we have a good cup of coffee."

Karen & David Moddrell

Main Street Coffee House sits on the old Independence Square. The Square itself has gone through a re-vitalization and Karen, the owner, wanted to be a part of that. She wanted to see more businesses, as well as more art, come to the Square, which is rich in history.

Karen's background is in theater, specifically set design and lighting, and you will quickly see that she supports all the arts. She promotes a different local artist each month by giving them the walls of the coffee shop as their private art gallery.

She also showcases local musicians with live music several evenings a month, and she invites local authors to host their book signings at her place.

Since Karen opened her coffee shop more than two years ago, she has seen several art galleries open nearby, and now there is an art crawl on the Square each month. Even if you're not from the area, this is a fun little outing to take and enjoy the historic part of the city, the art, and of course, the coffee. When you walk in the coffee shop, you will notice one of Karen's creations that we thought was cool—she collected old doors and doorknobs to make the counter.

CUPPING The method that professionals use to taste and evaluate coffee. Coffee is ground into an 8-oz. porcelain or glass cup, and water is poured on top of the coffee. The coffee steeps for a few minutes and the grinds rise to the top, forming a crust. The crust is broken with a silver spoon and the cupper evaluates the coffee's aromas, and after the coffee cools for a bit, the cupper slurps the liquid, evaluates the flavors, and spits the coffee out to avoid caffeine intake.

AMERICANO A shot or two of espresso that has been poured into a glass filled with hot water.

CAPPUCINO Cappuccino gets its name from the Italian order of Catholic Capuchin monks, whose hooded robes resemble the drink's cap of foam in shape and color. The frothed milk from the top of the steaming pitcher is spooned on top to "cap" the cappuccino and retain heat. The proportion of espresso to steamed and frothed milk for cappuccino is usually 1/3 espresso, 1/3 steamed milk, and 1/3 frothed milk on top.

ESPRESSO A brewing method invented in Italy at the turn of the century that extracts the heart of the bean. A pump-driven machine forces hot water through fine grounds at around nine atmospheres of pressure. It should take between 18 to 23 seconds to extract a good shot. This will produce from 3/4 to 1 ounce of great liquid—a sweet, thick and rich, smooth shot of espresso. Comes from the Latin word "Expresere" which means "to press out."

LATTE A shot or two of espresso that has been poured into a cup filled with steamed milk and topped off with foamed milk (about a 1/4").

MOCHA A small irregular bean which has a unique acid character. Generally shipped from Mocha Yemen or sometimes mixed with coffee shipped from Mocha Yemen. A Mocha drink is one that is made with coffee and cocoa.

This coffee house is in the old Muddy's place on 39th St., which you probably remember, but they gave it a much appreciated remodel and came out with a very cheery cafe feel. I have tried to stick primarily to basic coffee shops, but this is one exception I can't leave out. They have a creative menu and both the owners, Ted Habiger and Andrew Sloan, are chefs, but people really do come in just for the coffee. They have a complete espresso bar and baristas who can create your favorite coffee drink or Italian soda.

You really should check this place out for breakfast or lunch. I am truly awestruck over some of their creations. They have daily selections on the menu along with their standards. They use fresh produce from local farms and you can tell. Everything tastes as if it was just picked.

This coffee shop sits directly across from a train depot built in 1905. You can even catch the Amtrak train there still today. I love the small town feeling you get from walking around downtown Lee's Summit. I grew up in the area and think it's great that so many locally owned boutique businesses have come in and restored the old buildings. I remember buying candy as a little girl at the "Five and Dime", just a couple of doors down from here. Well, now that I have totally dated myself, let's talk coffee. This is the place to be. I love the deck out back and the big trees—I am pretty happy if I get coffee, and really happy if I get to drink it outside.

A large group of men seemed to be enjoying their coffee over some good conversation. I always seem to see more men in coffee shops with their friends than women. I think women need to slow down, smell the coffee, and spend more time in coffee shops talking to their friends. Vicki and Tom are not the original owners of the Whistle Stop, but used to be customers. When they heard there was an opportunity to buy it, they jumped. They loved the way the place looked as customers, so they changed very little. They have recently added a second location in Lakewood.

BARISTA Someone who makes coffee drinks as a profession.

ARABICA The better of the two primary types of coffee. Arabica is grown at higher altitudes, is less disease and pest-resistant, and yields less coffee per year, but has the nuance, liveliness (brightness), intensity, and variety of flavors prized by coffee lovers, with less caffeine. Arabica contains 1.1 percent compared to robusta's 2.2 percent.

DEMITASSE A small (1/2 size) cup used for serving espresso. It is a French term meaning 'half cup'.

FRENCH PRESS A device for making coffee in which ground coffee is steeped in water. The grounds are then removed from the coffee by means of a filter plunger which presses the grounds to the bottom of the pot. Also referred to as a plunger pot.

BECKI MCCRAY

Becki was looking for the right opportunity to get her out of the corporate world and out of a long commute each day. Becki's daughter, Sarah, planted the seed. Sarah had worked in a coffee shop during her college years and was deciding the corporate world might not be the place where she wanted to spend her life either. As Becki did her research she decided one of the most important factors she wanted to achieve was to create a feeling of the coffee shop being a community place. According to Becki, many suburbanites have gotten into a bad rut of opening their garage doors as they drive in and closing it before they ever get out of the car, which leaves little room for any interaction with neighbors. She was hoping for a place where people would stop before or after work to enjoy the company of others, over a cup of coffee.

The atmosphere changes on Friday and Saturday nights, with live music packing the place out with a younger crowd. If you are brave and have talent you'd like to share, there's open mic night once a month. You can check out their schedule online. Becki's older daughter has since moved, but her younger daughter, Stephanie, can be seen behind the counter making one of their many specialty coffee drinks. If you are wondering about the name, the coffee shop is named after Zoe, the McCrays' black Labrador.

David Ford

YJ'S
café
"Food That Does
A Body Good!"

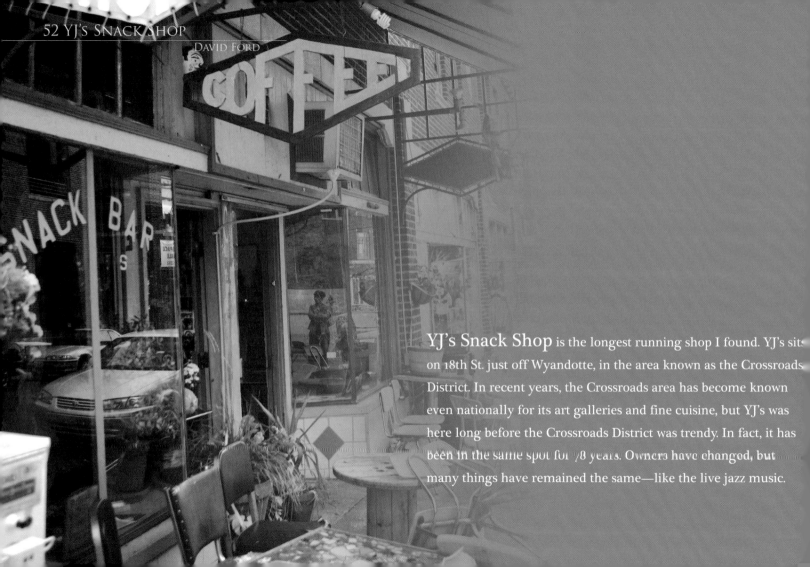

DAVID FORD

YJ's Snack Shop is the longest running shop I found. YJ's sits on 18th St. just off Wyandotte, in the area known as the Crossroads District. In recent years, the Crossroads area has become known even nationally for its art galleries and fine cuisine, but YJ's was here long before the Crossroads District was trendy. In fact, it has been in the same spot for 78 years. Owners have changed, but many things have remained the same—like the live jazz music.

I asked David when they had live music, he responded, "Whenever there is a hungry jazz musician." The little colorful shop offers hot daily specials as well as some standards. Even though the space is small, that doesn't stop it from bringing in a crowd. You will enjoy a mix of patrons—local artists hang out here as well as business people. The coffee shop is old-school. It doesn't serve decaf. Why bother. If you haven't dropped by YJ's, make the time. It's a fun stop.

JUDY & LANNY RIEDEL
CHRYSA & DAVID ZINSER

OK, we are in Kansas, but this coffee shop offers special recipes for vegans and people on gluten-free diets. If you are on a non-restricted diet, this is also the place to indulge, because they are creating some desserts that are unique to the coffee shop setting, like baklava—which I believe I could hear calling my name.

This is the place to come for a great cup of coffee because they roast their own beans and have some special blends like Black Cat and, for the holidays, Java Jingle. You can also spend some quality time with your laptop or a good book. In fact, one man has written 14 books right here. Toto's stays open late to accommodate students, bible studies, and special interest groups.

Toto's has been around for over 15 years and gone through quite a few changes. With Charles Gabauer as a managing partner, we are looking forward to him bringing his new ideas and culinary expertise to the table.

DANNY O'NEILL

The Roasterie comes from the kind of beginnings I think are always fun to hear about. It's the kind of story that makes you realize that with a dream and a lot of hard work, great things can happen.

In high school, Danny had the opportunity to live in Costa Rica as a foreign exchange student, and actually got to pick coffee beans in the mountains. Obviously never getting this out of his blood, he went along a different career path until he decided to go back to something he really loved. That's when he started his journey learning all about coffee and what it takes to start your own business. With a small roaster in the basement of his home, Danny founded The Roasterie in 1993. That's the story in a nutshell, but of course it didn't happen overnight or by accident. It was a lot of hard work, and Danny had the help of many good people. The story does not end there. I think the best part is the way Danny has given back to the communities in the countries where he buys beans, investing in the people to make their lives a little better.

Danny O'Neill

The Roasterie is open for public tours on Saturday mornings, which I would highly recommend if you are interested in coffee. My husband and I enjoyed it and gained a new appreciation for the people who go about the business of buying beans from the farmers, roasting the beans, and getting them to us so we can relax and have a great cup of coffee at home or at one of our favorite coffee shops. The people there were incredibly friendly and informative.

That brings me to the newest of Danny's ventures—he has opened a coffee shop in the Brookside area. He wanted to be in Brookside because that's where he started, and he loves the small neighborhood feel that still exists there today. He wanted to open this store to provide barista training and to keep in touch with the final consumer, which I think is important when you're in the wholesale business. You can sometimes forget who it is that you are ultimately working for.

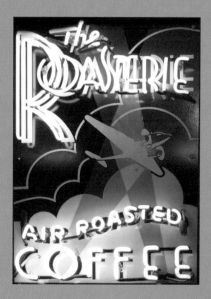

Huntley & Amy Parker

Beanology, is the the study of beans. Well, maybe not—in this case it is the name of a new coffee shop in South Overland Park. At the time of this writing, it is still under construction, and I look forward to checking it out. I found it interesting that this new shop's owners are going head to head with about three big guys that you can see from their parking lot. But if the old location, location, location rule holds true, I'm sure they will do quite well. They have a drive-thru, so if you're in a hurry or maybe still in your bathrobe on the way home from taking the kids to school, you can sneak a cup without getting out of your car.

The owners, Huntley and Amy Parker, admit to being very brave or just crazy. Well, we wish them luck with their new venture. I'm anxious to see their spot when it's all done. You can also check out their fun website, Beanology.com.

Coffee Bay
103rd and Pflumm, Lenexa, Ks   913 888 3001

By The Book
4 North Main, Liberty, Mo   816 792 3200

Broadway Café
4106 Broadway, Kansas City, Mo   816 531 2432
301 Westport Rd., Kansas City, Mo   816 931 9955
broadwaycafeandroastery.com

Parkville Coffee & Fudge
113 Main Street, Parkville, Mo   816 587 4200

Mildred's Coffeehouse
7921 Santa Fe Dr., Overland Park, Ks   913 341 0301
920 Main St., 2nd Floor, Kansas City, Mo   816 842 9115
1821 Wyandotte, Kansas City, Mo   816 471 1155
mildredscoffeehouse.com

City Market Coffeehouse
305 Main Street, Kansas City, Mo   816 718 3005
citymarketcoffeecompany.com

Hi Hat
5012 State Line Rd., Westwood Hills, Ks   913 722 5000
hihatcoffee.com

The Coffeehouse
738 N. 7 Highway, Blue Springs, Mo   816 229 7030

Hattie's Fine Coffee
4195 Somerset Dr., Prairie Village, Ks   913 648 2326
hattiesfinecoffee.com

Main Street Coffee House
107 S. Main, Independence, Mo   816 836 2633

Room 39
1719 West 39th Street, Kansas City, Mo   816 753 3939
rm39.com

Whistle Stop Coffee and Mercantile
227 SE Main, Lee's Summit, Mo   816 525 4545
929 NE Woods Chapel Rd., Lee's Summit, Mo   816 554 1345
whistlestopcoffee.com

Black Dog Coffeehouse
12815 W. 87th St. Pkwy., Lenexa, Ks   913 495 5515
bdcoffeehouse.com

YJ's Snack Bar
128 W. 18th Street, Kansas City, Mo   816 472 5533

Toto's Coffee
6915 Johnson Dr., Mission, Ks   913 722 2332

The Roasterie Cafe
6223 Brookside Blvd., Kansas City, Mo   816 333 9700
theroasterie.com

Beanology
7224 W. 135th St., Overland Park, Ks   913 239 8850
beanology.com

Bibliography

These sites were used in compiling facts, history, and definitions.

congacoffee.com

e-importz.com

nantucketcoffee.com

dunkindonuts.com

coffeehouse. Answers.com. The American Heritage® Dictionary of the English Language, Fourth Edition, HoughtonMifflin Company, 2004. http://www.answers.com/topic/coffeehouse.